Write, Publish, Sell!

Quick, Easy, Inexpensive Ideas
for the Marketing Challenged

Other Books by Valerie Allen

Beyond the Inkblots: Confusion to Harmony
Suffer the Little Children
Sins of the Father
Summer School for Smarties
Bad Hair, Good Hat, New Friends

Write, Publish, Sell!

Quick, Easy, Inexpensive Ideas
for the Marketing Challenged

by

Valerie Allen

Valerie Allen

Write, Publish, Sell!

Quick, easy, inexpensive ideas
for the marketing challenged

Copyright 2007 by Valerie Allen
Second Edition 2012 by Valerie Allen

ISBN 10: 1480043850
ISBN 13: 978 1480043855
Printed in the United States of America

Deepest Appreciation

Thank you to the National League of American Pen Women, The Space Coast Writers' Guild, and the Blueprints One Writers' Group for their support, encouragement, critiques, and edits of my work over the years. I believe publishing success is found in the words we write and the sincerity of those who help us along the way.

I am especially grateful to the readers and editors who shared their skills, talents, and support to make this book possible: Vista and Lee Boyland, Judith Mammay, and Jim Rootsey.

Valerie Allen
Melbourne, Florida

Write, Publish, Sell!   *Valerie Allen*

CONTENTS

- Categories of Children's Books
- Take Aim and Target Your Children's Writing

- Good Sentences: Word by Word
- Mighty Monosyllables
- Ol' Whatshisname!
- Pesky Pronouns
- Repetitive Redundancies
- Sentence *No Nos*
- Sentences: It's All in the Details
- Word Wise
- Writing Style: Syntactical Arrangement

INTRODUCTION

Different Skill Sets

There are three distinct skill sets involved in being a successful author: writing, publishing, and marketing.

Each of these require unique knowledge and tasks. As with all we do in life, we may be more adept at one skill than another.

We must write our own book. Publishing gives us the option of doing it ourselves or having it completely handled by someone else. Marketing will always have to be part of our personal success plan, involving the support of others. This leads us to make decisions about the investment of our effort, time, and money to become a successful author.

Writing

It is likely as you write, you will encounter errors, however, the more you write the better you will do. As with most things, practice brings improvement. You will also use your research skills to find information both about the art and craft of writing as well as the topic of your book. Persistence is the key to success.

Publishing

Typically, publication is not something most authors know much about. If you are fortunate enough to have a college degree, or work experience in this field, you have an advantage.

You will have to acquire some basic information about the different publication options available, each with their benefits and drawbacks.

You may decide publishing is something best left to those in that line of work. You may be able to learn and do what it takes to publish by yourself, but it will take time away from your writing and may not turn out as professional as you expected. You need to spend time exploring publishing options.

Marketing

Marketing leads to sales. Marketing is a marathon it is not a sprint. It is not one thing you do once in a while from which you have immediate or lasting results.

Marketing is a skill which you can learn and practice. Although you may have some marketing support from your publisher, as an author, you will have to market your work. To what extent you invest in marketing is your decision. However, every author comes to understand you must tell to sell.

CHAPTER 1

Writers Write

Writers write. This is a simple truth, but until you actually put words onto paper, you are not a writer.

You may think, ponder, read, study, research, interview, or discuss. Writers do all of these things. These are necessary, but not sufficient to be a writer. Writers must write.

Persistence:the Key to Success

You must write often. It's likely you write each day, but don't realize it. Have you sent an email, made a grocery list, designed an action plan at work, completed a form, written a letter, put a note inside a birthday card? All of these count toward your daily writing quota, but each of these missives take you in a different writing direction.

Some writing is fun, some required. Some writing uses proper grammatical form, some less formal, some must be typed, some completed in pencil, or blue ink. Some writing is enjoyable, some is not.

All writing does one thing: it forces you to put your thoughts into words. If you have a story to tell, fiction, nonfiction, or in poetic form, you must transform your thoughts into words and then put them onto paper. When you do this, you are truly a writer.

Five-Minutes-A-Day Writing Plan

There are 24 hours—1,440 minutes—in each day. How valuable are five of

16

these 1,440 minutes in your day? Are you willing to invest five minutes a day to achieve your writing goals? If you want to be a writer, step one is: you must write.

During your five-minutes-a-day exercise, you must write continuously. Find a place to be alone (this may be your first challenge!). Set a timer for five minutes. Whether with pen and paper or keyboard and computer, set aside five minutes of uninterrupted writing time just for you. Out of the 1,440 minutes available each day, surely you are entitled to have five of these minutes for yourself.

Let your mind wander as your fingers do the writing. This is a time to be creative. No editing, no concerns about spelling, no grammar rules—just let the words flow from brain cells to fingertips.

At first, your writing may be a rant about the laundry, an unfinished project, family issues, hassles at work, the price of gas, or the state of world. That's fine. Keep writing. If words don't come, start to doodle. Circles are very soothing! Keep the pen to the paper or fingers to the keyboard. Stay physically connected to your writing.

Make lists of things to do, names of old friends, places you've lived, people you've loved, cars you've owned, pets you've had, foods you hate. Just keep writing. Describe things around you, write about a favorite place, tell about a person you love, an event you enjoyed. This daily writing exercise is a time of introspection, a connection with your inner self, to enjoy free flowing thoughts. Keep writing.

As you do this daily five minutes of continuous writing, you'll find relief from mundane and querulous day-to-day life events. The creative part of your brain will free your muse. The child inside will begin to play, to experiment, to enjoy, to laugh, and liberate you from the critical editor stifling your creativity. As you write, you will enrich your thoughts and stimulate your vocabulary. You will become a better writer.

Writer's Block
vs.
Plumber's Block

What is holding you back from following your writing dreams? Time, money, family responsibilities, employment obligations?

Do you have a case of the *wait untils*? I'll wait until: *I graduate, Get a job, Have a better job, Save more money, Pay off the car, Find more time, The kids start school, The kids finish school, I retire.* Sound familiar?

To quote a famous writer, "The saddest words of mouth and pen are those that say what might have been." If you wait until you find the perfect moment, you may live a long, but unpublished life.

Authors often speak of "writer's block." It's described as a blank mind, deplete of ideas, or the inability to think of anything to write.

Now try to have a blank mind. Sit quietly and try hard not to think about anything. Didn't work did it? No, it didn't and it won't. Your mind cannot go blank. Your mind is always working and thinking.

Medical research tells us even during sleep, when we are not consciously aware of thought, our brains are still going strong. As long as we're alive, our brain is producing thought. When our brain stops, we're legally dead.

19

Writer's block doesn't mean our brains won't work. It means we cannot force our thoughts into words. We cannot seem to form the words we want for our book, story, or poem.

Have faith. Your brain is working, even while you are engaged in other activities. Suddenly, the thoughts will begin to flow. Be ready. Have paper and pen at all times, in all places to capture those fleeting ideas, words, and phrases before they escape.

For those who use the excuse of "writer's block" to keep from writing, I have a question. Have you ever heard of plumber's block, dentist's block, teacher's block, or accountant's block? Are writers the only professionals to suffer from this functional limitation? Writers are not blocked by anything. Writers write.

Find Your Passion

All writing falls into three broad categories: fiction, nonfiction or poetry. You may dabble in all three or put your efforts into just one genre. To be a successful writer, find what you love and enjoy. Find the thing you can write about with passion, with urgency, with a nagging need to get it done, and persevere. A writer is obsessed with the need to compose. A writer may find it both frustrating and liberating.

Writers tend to view the world differently. They experience life and wonder about it at the same time. They can stand outside the event and ponder cause and effect. Writers think in 'what ifs' and 'supposes.' They don't just hear, they listen carefully for the well-crafted use of words, turn of a phrase, and unique expressions. Writers describe by comparison, they give particulars, and they use details. Writers paint a picture with words.

Don't Quit the Day Job

For the chosen few who write a bestseller or blockbuster and make millions of dollars, there is no need to worry about finances. Money will flow from what you love doing; for the rest of us—keep the day job.

On the journey to published author, most writers have another career, which they keep even after publishing success. The day job is your insurance, your financial security, your baby blanket. It provides you with funds, respectability, and yes, writing ideas.

Writing is a career that doesn't necessitate years of schooling and a large financial investment to become successful. It would be helpful if you had a degree in the fine arts, creative writing, journalism or English, but it's not required. You don't need to spend thousands of dollars on higher education to become a good writer.

It would be great to have a state-of-the-art computer (and know how to use it), but it's not necessary. Pen and paper have done nicely for hundreds of years.

You don't need a private office, few writers have one. A table in the kitchen, library, coffee shop, or park works as well as the desk of a CEO.

What you must have is persistence. What you must do is write.

CHAPTER 2

Doing it Right

In your enthusiasm to publish your book, there are some guidelines that will enhance your chances of doing it properly the first time.

Rules of the Game

As with any enterprise, the publishing world has industry standards. These rules change from time to time, but if you are seeking publication, you'll do better to follow the rules than to rile against them. You can always make exceptions later.

Standard practice is to use a computer. You may enjoy, be more creative, and feel comfortable writing by hand. Many authors feel more connected to their writing. This is fine, but ultimately your book must be typed into a standard computerized program.

If you write in longhand be prepared to spend time and money to have your work typed into a word processing program. You can do this yourself, find a friend or relative to do it for you, or pay to have it done.

It is likely you will need to watch for mistakes during the rewriting of your work. Errors can also occur when changing from one computer to another, one word processing program to another, or saving from one computer file to another. Computers are very efficient, but can be frustrating when they seem to have a mind of their own!

Every writer needs to be aware of the most common standards in the publishing industry:

- Your name and book title on the top of each page (use the *Header* feature)
- Double space all writing

- One inch margins on all sides
- 12 point type
- Simple   fonts(Courier,   New Times Roman, Arial)
- Center titles and captions
- Justified text
- Justify the first paragraph of each chapter, all other paragraphs are indented
- One space after a period
- Dialogue requires quotation marks ("Where are you?")
- Start a new paragraph with each different speaker
- Keep speaker action and dialogue in the same paragraph ("I'm here," Valerie said, and waved her hand in the air.)
- Statements tell and have a period at the end of the sentence. In dialogue use a comma inside the quotation and a period at the end of the sentence. "This is my book," Valerie said.
- Questions ask and have a question mark at the end of the sentence. In dialogue the question mark goes inside the quotation and the period is

used at the end of the sentence. "Where is my book?" Valerie asked.

- Subject verb sentence structure ("This is important," Valerie said. NOT: "This is important," said Valerie.)
- For time sequence use both words: *and then* (USE: She picked up a pen, and then wrote a note. NOT: She picked up a pen, then wrote a note.)
- Punctuation marks go inside quotation marks ("Here I am," Valerie said. "Where are you?")
- Numbers one through ten are spelled out, as is any number that begins a sentence.
- Numerals are used for numbers of three or more words (156); addresses, dates, exact money, and time
- An apostrophe replaces a missing letter (goin', don't, I'll)
- Use italics for internal character thoughts (*He never*

really loved me. He just wanted my money.)

- Use italics for titles of books and magazines
- Use italics to emphasize a word or phrase (*Help!*)
- Put a comma before *but* in a sentence (Valerie went, but I stayed home.)
- Limit the use of exclamation points, please!
- Use simple words to express complex ideas
- Avoid clichés
- Show, don't tell a character's emotions
  (Use: He clenched his fists, the veins in his neck pulsed, and sweat glistened on his forehead. Not: He was angry.)
- Avoid over-use of *that*
- Avoid redundancies (He shrugged. Not: He shrugged his shoulders.)
- Use dissimilar character names (Not: James, Jim, Joe, Jason, John, Jon; Mary, Marie, Marge, Molly)
- Facts must be accurate—especially dates, timelines,

directions, names of people and places
- Accuracy of clothing, cars, and other items for the time period (there were no laptops in 1960)
- Use a dash between multiword modifiers (twelve-year-old boy, well-kept secret, etc.)
- Bibliographies aren't always required, but keep notes of references and page numbers for documentation of unique information

Book Length

Non-fiction books are content-driven. The number of pages differs with the book style and content, for example, a child's alphabet picture book, a textbook, or an instruction manual. Non-fiction writing has specific information to relay to the reader with a more exact beginning and ending point. Examples of non-fiction include a flier, brochure, booklet, biography, self-help, or reference book.

The average fiction book for the adult reader is between 50,000 to 100,000 words. Although many are less and many are more, most novels fall within this number of words.

Using a standard 12-point font, there are approximately 250 words per page. A typical novel is between 250 to 350 pages in a book size approximately six inches by nine inches. The trend is books with fewer words and pages.

Covers and Spines

The front cover must sell your book. It must invite the readers' attention, encourage them to select your book, get them to hold it in their hands, move them to flip through the pages, and help them decide to buy. A daunting task for a book cover!

Browse in bookstores, and observe patrons as they scan books. How long do they view the cover before placing the book back on the shelf or carrying it to the checkout? Research shows it is 30 seconds or less.

The front cover must be clear and convey the theme of your book. With non-fiction, this is usually straightforward information and often has a sub-title to provide details that are more specific.

A fiction title can be misleading. For this reason, the book cover is even more important to convey the story concept.

The two most prominent parts of your book cover are the book title and your name. The title should be easily read from a distance of three feet. The best colors for a book cover are red, black, and golden-yellow.

The cover of your book is the first step to get the attention of a buyer. Unless you are an expert in graphics or photography, it is well worth your time and money to hire a professional to design your book cover or allow the publisher to do so.

If your book passes the front cover test, the reader will turn the book over to scan the back cover. This is a good sign.

The back cover should continue the color scheme and story theme. It should have the book title, your name, the story summary, reviews or quotes. Additionally, the back cover displays the ISBN, price, and bar code.

Also on the back cover, the book title and your name can be imbedded in the graphic or as a header or footer. The back cover is the place to add something significant about yourself, your experience, or your credentials to boost your credibility as an author.

This is the place for your photo. Unless it is a memoir, use a current picture. The background in the photo can lend itself to further you or your book theme. Try not to date yourself with clothing, jewelry, or hairstyle. These will make an impression on the reader as well, so choose carefully.

Books with the front cover facing out attract more attention; however, most books are displayed spine out toward the prospective buyer. The wider the spine, the easier it is to read. The spine should have the book title, your name and the publisher's name or logo.

When designing the outer parts of your book, remember, white space sells. It's easier for the reader to find details about you and your book if the information is widely spaced between each paragraph and block of text. An exterior crowded with text, graphics, and bright color can create visual overload.

Rejection

The ugly "R" word—rejection. After slaving over your writing, you will reach, *"The End."* It's difficult to let it go, to put your book out there and face possible rejection. It's hard to let your baby go forth into the big world, but a manuscript neatly packed in a box under your bed is not going to sell.

Part of every writer's life is the "R" word. Watching those rejection form letters pile up can be discouraging. Before giving up, consider these points of reference. Did you hop on your two-wheeler bike for the first time and take off on a smooth ride? Did you tie your shoes properly the first time? Did you win your first spelling bee? Probably not.

It's unrealistic to think your manuscript will be accepted 'as is' by the first agent or publisher who reads it. More likely, your final draft will need corrections, editing, rewrites, and multiple submissions.

The reasons for rejection of your manuscript are numerous, but tend to fall into certain patterns.

There may be legitimate literacy concerns. The story may be poorly written, grammatically incorrect, contain spelling errors or have point-of-view confusion. The plot may not be fully developed or lack tension. The story may be too short or too long to hold the readers' attention. The characters may be stereotyped, one dimensional, or without depth of emotion.

These are the easiest variables for you to control. Your willingness to accept feedback, edit, rewrite, correct, and update your manuscript will generally result in tighter and improved writing. The writer can control for literacy problems by improving his or her writing skills. Your writing will improve as you read more, attend writers' conferences, join a critic group, participate in writers' groups, and of course, write, write, write.

The political context of your book can also lead to rejection. There may be a glut of science fiction, horror, or love stories on the market at the time of your submission. The publisher may have another similar book about to be published and doesn't want to create undue competition. A publishing house can change their focus from Westerns to Romance. You have no control over these issues; however, diligent research will help you find the right fit for your book. If you believe in your story and feel it is worthy of publication, remember, persistence is the key to success.

Most frustrating for any author is the rejection of a well-written story, with intriguing characters, and an exciting plot. You have no doubt read many books and wondered how they ever found a publisher. Your book is so much better!

Keep in mind famous authors faced rejection many times before they found publication. For example, John Creasey wrote 564 books under 13 pseudonyms and received over 700 rejections. *The Good Earth* by Pearl S. Buck had 12 rejections before it was accepted for publication. James Joyce had over 20 rejections for *Dubliners*. J.K. Rowling, the wealthiest and most successful author of all time, had the Harry Potter story rejected time after time.

Remember also, even after literary success, six figure retainers, and fame that spread from book to screen, there are people who don't like to read works by Stephen King, John Grisham, Nora Roberts, Danielle Steel, John Steinbeck or Ernest Hemmingway. They have all suffered "reader rejection" at some point in their careers. When dealing with rejection, believe in yourself, be realistic, and keep things in perspective.

CHAPTER 3

The Push to Publish

After the final words are written, what to do next? Move on to publication. As many writers have discovered having your book published can take longer than getting your book written. It can also be a long and frustrating game of "wait and see."

Publishing Choices

There are four basic ways to publish your book: traditional

publishing, self-publication, print-on-demand(POD) and electronic. Each has advantages and disadvantages.

Traditional Publishing

Large publishing houses with extensive contracts and a marketing budget are referred to as traditional or mainstream publishers. Many are located in New York however, there are small publishing houses throughout the country as well as university presses associated with colleges. Traditional publishing houses buy the rights to publish your work, offer you a contract, including an advance, and specific marketing.

Few large publishers will accept unagented work. You must first research agents who are interested in the type of book you have written. Next, you write a concise one-page cover letter, asking if the agent would be interested in representing you and your work.

The cover letter must be powerful and succinct. It will introduce you, summarize your manuscript, and tell why you think it's a good fit for their literary agency.

Now be ready to wait. Typically, the waiting period runs from three to six months, perhaps longer, to hear from an agent. Then be prepared for a rejection form letter. If you are fortunate, the agent may offer you a reason for his or her lack of interest in your work. Consider this a bonus. You can learn from this feedback. If several agents offer similar comments, take it seriously and consider some revision of your work.

If an agent has an interest in your manuscript, he or she will request additional information. This may include a lengthy summary or the first few chapters of your book. If they are still interested after reviewing these materials, the agent will request a copy of your completed manuscript for review.

If the agent decides to represent you and your work, you will be offered a contract for a specific time period during which the agent will shop your book around to publishers. The contract should also specify the agent's percentage from your book sales, if and when they are able to find a publisher. Agents shouldn't charge you for their representation services. Agents make their money as a percentage of your book sales. Credible agents know which publishers are interested in which genre and waste no time in connecting with these publishing houses. Agents work on commission and are highly motivated to have a publisher accept your work. No one makes money until your book begins to sell.

Your agent will negotiate a contract with the publisher and protect your interests in various publishing rights and all matters related to publication of your book. This could include the printed book, e-book, audio, CD, media productions, movie rights, foreign rights, and so on.

Before you sign a contract with an agent or publisher, you should consult with an attorney who specializes in intellectual properties. After you have a contract with your publisher, it can take up to three years or longer for you to see your book in print.

There are three primary advantages of traditional publishing. They have an established readership. There are no costs to the writer. They do some initial marketing. Rule of thumb is that 80% of their marketing budget goes to 20% of the authors in a given publishing house. The drawbacks of traditional publishing are the long and unpredictable journey to see your book in print and low royalties.

Self-Publishing

Many authors turn to self-publishing, sometimes referred to as "vanity publishing," as a second option. This is especially popular for family histories, a collection of poems, children's stories, cookbooks for fundraisers or books intended for a limited number of specific readers, such as coworkers, travelers, or hobby groups. Organizations also use this option for publishing gift books for new or loyal customers.

Self-publishing gives you total control over all aspects of the book design, pages, book size, pricing, and publication date. You do not need an agent or a publisher. You write, buy, store, market, distribute, sell, and mail the books.

The primary drawback is cost. You work directly with a printer and negotiate the cost of printing your book based on quality and quantity. Typically, the more books (units) you have printed, the lower the unit cost per book, thus more profit margin for you. Obtaining the copyright, ISBN, Library of Congress Number, and so on is up to you. Marketing, sales and

required   accounting   are   your
responsibility.

The primary advantage is having
control over the process, time line,
and after paying printing and related
costs, all profits from book sales are
yours. The drawback to self-publishing
is the skill, time, and money you must
commit to the process—all of which
takes time away from your writing.

Print On Demand (POD)

Print-on-Demand has become more
popular in recent years. For a minimal
cost, POD publishers afford the writer
an opportunity to have a professionally
published book, maintain control over
his or her work, and keep copyright
ownership. As a book is ordered, it is
printed so there is no outlay of funds
to publish hundreds of books at one
time and no need for storage.

A healthy competition has arisen
among   new   and   established   POD
publishers resulting in costs becoming
more   reasonable.   POD   publishers
typically bundle various services for a
flat rate cost to the author. This may
include   typesetting,   cover   design,
obtaining the ISBN, Library of Congress
number,   listing   it   with   book

distributors, listing it with online booksellers, limited marketing, and exposure in catalogs. Typically, the more you pay, the more services you receive.

Authors using POD publishers can purchase their own books at a discount and set up marketing and direct sales to increase their profit margin. If you do not want to be involved in direct sales, the POD, bookstores, and online venues will sell the books and royalties will be paid to the author on a quarterly basis.

Consider whether you have the marketing skills and want to invest time and money in POD publishing. Even if you are capable of maneuvering through the publishing process, it will divert time from your writing. Cost to the author and lack of marketing are the two main drawbacks of POD publishing.

Another consideration when choosing a publishing venue is chain bookstores are not always willing to give shelf space to non-traditionally published work.

Electronic Publishing

A fast growing option is electronic online publishing. This includes hard cover, paper back, and electronic books. This is relatively inexpensive and efficient. You write your book, create a cover, and convert it to an online format based on the requirements of the E-publisher you are using. Some E-publishers also have programs to create your own cover using a variety of templates, designs, and fonts.

Additional benefits are updates, corrections, and new editions are quickly and easily done. You simply type in your new material and upload your book again. Typically there is no cost involved in this do-it-yourself updating of material.

The benefit is the author has total control over the content, cover design, and the publication date. The royalties are considerably higher than any other form of publication. You can also have your book converted into an electronic book for various reader formats.

A drawback of E-publishing is that it does take some advanced computer skills. However, E-publishers typically have a step-by-step tutorial for the do-it-yourself option. If you feel less than confident to enter into the world of computer publishing, the E-publisher will do it for you at relatively low cost. You can also hire someone who is computer savvy to do the work for you.

The overall choice for publishing your book boils down to consideration of time vs. money.

Chapter 4

The Five Essentials

Five basic pieces of information must be available for the potential buyer: your name, book title, your 25-word pitch, a tag line from the book, and a business card.

The first four items should appear on all of your promotional materials. Your business card should be readily available without digging in your purse or wallet.

If you are using your computer to make fliers, order forms, or any printed matter, insert a header with your name, book title and ISBN. If using a logo, insert this as well. You want name recognition to enhance sales of this book and the next and the next.

Your Name

How lucky for the writer named Aaron Able—always at the top of the list, always on the first shelf. There are also those logo-lucky people with picture-word names, such as, Butler, Flowers, MacIntosh, Strawberry, or Weaver. If you are not so fortunate, take heart. Many writers with end-of-the-alphabet names, those too difficult to pronounce, or with a negative connotation have found publishing success.

Authors strive for name recognition. You want to become established as an author people are interested in knowing more about. You want to be so well known readers look forward to reading your next book regardless of the title or content.

Current authors, such as John Grisham, James Patterson, Nora Roberts, and Roxanne St. Clair have a following. Readers sign up well in advance to buy the next book by these authors. These writers have proven they can consistently satisfy their readers. These authors have name recognition, something you need to strive toward.

Book Title

Stories abound regarding the author's choice of book titles. Big-name-traditional publishing houses actually refer to the original title as a "working title." The publishing house typically makes creative title changes, some are a total replacement and others a slight change. In some cases these changes seem to have made a difference in the bottom line—big sales.

Explore your title with friends and family. Does the title tell or imply what the book is about? One of the benefits of membership in a writers' group is to get feedback about the impact the title has on them. Consider whether the title sets up the story or confuses the reader. Does your title have a hidden or double meaning?

You can look on line to find books with the exact same title. It is also useful to search for similar book titles or those using some of the same words. For example, if your title is *Magic Night*, search for that exact title. Also look for *A Magical Night*, *The Magic Night*, *That Magic Night*, *A Night of Magic*, *Another Night of Magic*, and so on.

Remember, book titles cannot have a copyright. In addition to online book sellers, you can check on the number of books with the same title through your library database and by using the Worldwide Card Catalog at www.worldwidecat.org.

Your 25 Word Pitch

A 25-word pitch for your book is no easy task, but it must be done. This is the essence of what your book is about—a *very condensed version*. This is your elevator speech.

Imagine being in a crowded elevator with your book in hand and the person next to you asks what your book is about. The elevator provides a captive audience to generate interest in you and your book, but only for the time it takes to get from one floor to the next.

Don't think you can boil your book down to twenty-five words? Your book is too long, your story too complex?

Glance through movie listings and bestseller lists. A two-hour movie or a

400-page book is cleverly reduced to one or two sentences.

Here is a quiz. How many of these story pitches can you match with the movie or book?

1. Caped Crusader goes against the Penguin and Catwoman

2. Firefighting siblings search for an arsonist

3. Mysterious assassin hired by a Russian gangster to kill a prominent American

4. An Hawaiian orphan girl adopts a precocious alien pet

5. Young lawyer takes on an insurance company

6. Teen learns a murderous wizard has escaped from jail

7. Parents try to manage careers while raising 12 children

8. Archaeologist tries to locate the Ark of the Covenant, while fighting Nazis, tarantulas, and snakes

9. Separated twins meet at camp, change places and hatch a plot to reunite their divorced parents

10. Independent women struggle to establish first pro-baseball league

11. Married lawyer's fling brings death and destruction

49

12. Young, beautiful, but belligerent Southern Belle finds bitterness and love during civil war era

> (Find the answers at the end of the chapter.)

Wonder how they did it? There is a definite pattern to these story pitches. Use your book and try this exercise to write an enticing 25-word pitch.

1. Adjective (Amazing)
2. Protagonist (bird watcher)
3. Action (discovers)
4. Goal (flying pigs)
5. Outcome (overcomes resistance of the scientific community and wins a lifetime supply of free bacon!)

Just as with your book, your 25-word pitch will be written and rewritten many times before it sounds right, captures the essence of your story, and easily rolls off your tongue during those elevator moments.

Tag Line

Some say the difference between a good book and a great book is a line remembered long after the book has been forgotten. Famous one-liners have worked their way into our language as clichés. A phrase or single sentence often comes to represent a belief or concept. The title of the movie or book may escape us, but the tag line plays on in our memory.

Try to find the essential truth in your book and reduce it to one sentence. Read your story and hunt for the one line that seems to convey your message to the reader.

To see how effective a tag line is, try to match these famous tag lines to a movie or book.

A. Frankly, my dear, I don't give a damn.
B. I'm going to make him an offer he can't refuse.
C. Toto, I've got a feeling we're not in Kansas anymore.
D. Here's looking at you, kid.
E. Go ahead, make my day.
F. May the Force be with you.
G. Love means never having to say you're sorry.
H. The stuff that dreams are made of.
I. E.T. phone home.
J. They call me Mr. Tibbs!

K. I'm as mad as hell, and I'm not going to take this anymore!
L. Show me the money!
M. I'll be back.
(Find the answers at the end of the chapter.)

Business Card Budget

A "must have" for a professional author is a business card. No one should ever wonder who you are or how to get in touch with you.

Minimal information on your business card includes your name, book title, email address, and web page. Additionally, you may include the ISBN, a post office box, or FAX number for direct book sales. To avoid unexpected company, do not use your physical address on your business card.

The reverse side of your business card can be used for promotional ideas and other information. This is the place for your photo or book cover. It's also a great spot to interest your reader with that 25-word pitch or tag line from your book. You can also list your other book titles. Other suggestions are ordering information, awards, a discount, a bonus gift, contest or an offer of free mailing.

A low-budget idea is to rubber stamp a small picture that coincides with your story or your name on the face of your card. Craft shops have hundreds of unique stamps with letters, numbers, symbols, plants, animals, smiley faces, etc.

Business cards will likely be the least expensive item in your marketing plan, but the most versatile. Hand them to others when introduced. Keep them in your car, wallet, purse, briefcase, home, and office. Use them as bookmarks in each of your books. Leave them in shopping carts and in restaurants. Enclose them in the envelop when paying bills or making bank deposits by mail.

QUIZ ANSWERS

25-Word Summaries:
1. *Batman Returns*
2. *Backdraft*
3. *The Jackal*
4. *Lilo and Stitch*
5. *The Rainmaker*
6. *Harry Potter & the Prisoner Azkaban*
7. *Cheaper by the Dozen*
8. *Raiders of the Lost Ark*
9. *The Parent Trap*

10. *A League of Their Own*
11. *Fatal Attraction*
12. *Gone With the Wind*

Famous Tag Lines:

   A. *Gone With the Wind*
   B. *The Godfather*
   C. *The Wizard of Oz*
   D. *Casablanca*
   E. *Sudden Impact*
   F. *Star Wars*
   G. *Love Story*
   H. *The Maltese Falcon*
   I. *E.T. The Extra-Terrestrial*
   J. *In the Heat of the Night*
   K. *Network*
   L. *Jerry Maguire*
   M. *The Terminator*

CHAPTER 5

Hunting for the Perfect Reader

Regardless of how you choose to publish your work, marketing is up to you. Traditional, commercial publishers have a marketing plan and a budget to support it, however, their seasoned authors typically get the lion's share. Some POD publishers have marketing packages you can buy, which include a variety of promotional and public relations options. If you self-publish, marketing is completely your responsibility.

Your Target Audience

Two popular beliefs are of interest when developing your marketing plan. Whether valid or not, it is said 70% of book purchases are made by women and the best read individuals in the United States are educators, attorneys, and librarians. You want to appeal to these identified groups.

Hunting vs. Fishing

There are two types of book buyers: those who hunt for books and those who fish for books.

Hunters are looking specifically for you, your book, or your topic. They have a vested interest in you or the type of book you have written. They know what they are looking for and actively seek it out. They ask the reference librarian for what they want. They search bookstores, go online, participate in Friends-of-the-Library book sales, and join book clubs. They are hunting for you and your book to be educated or entertained.

These book hunters may focus on a particular genre or author. They may enjoy science fiction, military books, or romance. They may follow a specific author regardless of the book title or content. This is especially true for those interested in nonfiction. An individual who wants to know about World War II, how to make ice cream, or names of great inventors, will seek out books specific to their interests.

Those who fish throw out the net and catch what they can. They read from the bestseller lists, a friend's suggestion, books new in the library, books featured in a press release, books by local authors, or a book won as a door prize. They will find treasured books at thrift stores and rummage sales. They enjoy expanding their reading horizons and are open to new authors and experiences. They are fishing and will read whatever book they happen to catch.

Your Ideal Readers

Who are your ideal readers? Hunters. Who would see or hear about you or your book and stop what they're doing or go out of their way to make a purchase? Hunters. They are your ideal readers. Imagine filling a convention center room with row after row of people who want to read your book. What would these people look like? What would they be wearing? What level of education would they have? What is their economic status? What would their interests be? Nail down your ideal reader and market with these people in mind.

Hunters are your first buyers and most important to your sales success. They will enjoy your book and share it with others. They will spread the word. They will go out hunting for your book and tell others when they have found it.

Your secondary buyers are fishing for a book. They are in the mood to read a good book and will pick up whatever is available.

These people may have a passing interest in you or your topic or story. They buy your book in response to the suggestion of a friend, an enticing book display, or good sale price. They may be impulse buyers who make a gift purchase on their way to visit a friend, family member, or coworker. These secondary buyers enjoy your book, discuss it with others, give it to a friend, or donate it to a book club. They are also important to build your fan base and reach more potential buyers.

Identify your 'hunters.' Find your perfect reader and capitalize on the innate bond you have with that individual to drive your first marketing efforts. Here are things you need to know and do to find these people and make a connection.

Tell to Sell

Your book may be the next best-seller, but it could wind up being a well-kept secret. You and your book have to be known to as many people as possible. More importantly, you want your book in the hands of people connected to many other people. People with credibility. People who can influence others with their reading suggestions. People who can persuade others to buy your book.

The Rule of 150

People do business with people they know. How many people do you know? According to some research, about 150. These people hear your name and know who you are. This includes family members, in-laws, and ex-in-laws. They can be part of your current life such as neighbors, friends or coworkers.

They may be from your past: friends from school or college, your old neighborhood, previous employment, clubs, volunteer organizations, PTA, or your child's soccer team.

Each of these 150 people will be your connection to their 150 people. It may seem crowded, but this is what you need for word of mouth promotion.

Make and Grow Your List

Go ahead, make a list. Start with family, friends, coworkers and neighbors. The current day-to-day people in your life. Not to 150 yet?

It is likely you had a life before you got this job, lived in this neighborhood, and married into a new family. Who are all those people? This is your opportunity to reacquaint yourself with friends, previous coworkers, schoolmates and others you used to know. Let them see how far you've come.

Now, add nodding acquaintances to your list. The people you pass with a friendly hello, the letter carrier, the checkout clerk, the dental assistant, those you sit next to you in the employee lounge, at homeowners' meetings, or people you see at your child's baseball game.

Have you gotten to 150 yet? Keep thinking. Each time you meet or speak with someone, you can add him or her to your list of 150. Best practice is to hand them your business card. Ask for his or her email address for follow-up, and for future reference, note the date and where you met. Add their email address to your online mailing list.

Electronic Friends

In the ever expanding world of online friends, your contacts are limitless. Your live friends are people you know face-to-face. These are real people currently part of your life or perhaps from your past.

Your *E* friends can include your live friends, but can expand to hundreds or thousands more. *E* friends have been established through social networking. These people know you via your online profile. These are people you have met through email, Twitter, My Space, Facebook, blogs, and similar online venues. If you want to be a big selling author, you must be part of the electronic highway.

CHAPTER 6

Wherever You Go There You Are

Ever wonder about this thing called "name recognition?" Politicians, professional athletes, musicians, artists, movie stars, and TV journalists all know the power of name recognition.

Is it important to writers? You bet. Aside from current popular writers, such as K.J. Rowling and Toni Morrison, these accomplished scribes linger on as well: Harper Lee, Ernest

Hemingway, John Steinbeck, William Faulkner, Jane Austen, and Pearl S. Buck.

You too, want and need name recognition to reach beyond your list of 150 live friends and your extended file of E friends.

Your Tipping Point

An interesting book by Malcolm Gladwell, *The Tipping Point*, describes three types of individuals crucial to putting you and your product or service over the top—the tipping point.

Gladwell calls the first type of person a *Connector*. This person knows many other people. He's connected to others through organizations, volunteer work, employment, hobbies, and professional associations. This person knows, sees, and talks with many people on a regular basis.

The second type of person Gladwell identifies is a *Maven*. These people have lots of information and freely offer it to others. They are looking to share their wealth of knowledge with other deserving people. They want to help others save money, improve their health, move up in their career, invest wisely, or marry the right person. They are helpful people with lots of information about many things of interest to others and are eager to share.

The third type of person Gladwell calls the *Salesperson*. This individual is so intrigued by a product or service he easily convinces others of its value and benefits. He is able to clearly summarize the pros and cons and weigh in on the side of the pros. He persuades others to buy and feel good about their purchase.

How many people on your list of 150 can you identify as a *Connector*, *Maven*, or *Salesperson*? You need all three of these types of people to move your book up to and over the tipping point of multiple sales.

You in the News

There is more than one way to see your name in print. You can put your name and the name of your book in the hands of hundreds of people for free. It's easy.

Does your high school or college seek tidbits for alumni news? Does your church have a bulletin with news about congregation members? Does your professional or home owner association have a newsletter?

These are all avenues of free publicity. These people are seeking news about members. What is more impressive than to have a published author in their midst?

Of course, add to this all your social networking efforts. You and your book should be showing up online on a weekly basis. You accomplish this by joining and being active in social groups related to your book topic.

Your online posts do not always have to be directly about your book. It is just as effective to have your name appear with a logo or thumbnail of your book cover. You can comment on the posts others have made. You can note seasonal events related to your book topic. You can offer writing tips. You can suggest a helpful web site. You can mention a book of interest to authors. You can write a guest blog. The marketing opportunities for reaching others online is limitless.

Your Media Kit

Your media kit is like a portable dog and pony show—about you and your book. You need to create a package that opens like a birthday-box surprise. The materials in your media kit represent you at your best. Media kits are usually given away free to journalists, radio and television hosts, organization directors, book reviewers, librarians, and others who are in a position to promote and share your book.

Media kits involve cost and creativity. In addition to the basics listed below, you should have a unique item that ties into the theme of your book.

Children's writers may include coloring books, fancy pencils, stickers, and similar items using characters from their book. A business book may include sticky notes with the book title across the top. An inspirational book of poems may have note cards with a thought for the day.

A basic media kit should contain:
- Your book
- A cover letter
- A fact sheet including:
  o ISBN
  o Publisher
  o Cover price
  o Format and size
  o Number of pages
  o Category of book

  o Publication date
  o Distributor
  o Your 25 words
  o Ordering information
- About the Author biography
- Reviews from print or online sources
- Business cards
- Book marks
- Posters
- A gift item unique to your book

The Press Release

Newspapers are always seeking people for hometown news. They want to know about local people doing things of interest. You do not have to do something extraordinary just something unique or of interest to others in your community.

Upon publication of your book, send a press release. If you have a claim to fame not specifically related to your book, be sure your book is mentioned as another accomplishment.

Here are some examples:
- John Doe, author of (your book title), is a volunteer for the ABC Youth Basketball

Team. Mr. Doe helps young athletes . . .

- John Doe, a local dentist and author of (title of your book), made a career day presentation at ABC Middle School on . . .

- John Doe, a long time resident of our town, and author of (title of your book), has just returned from a trip to Alaska where he . . .

- John Doe, a member of the local Chamber of Commerce and author of (title of your book), has been appointed to the landscape committee . . .

- John Doe, a retired motorcycle mechanic and author of (title of your book), is a member of the Friends of the Library Association. Mr. Doe helped set up the book sale, . . .

If your book ties in with a current movie, local event, or

celebration, point this out in your press release. For example, if you have a homeless individual in your novel, November would be a likely time to get some publicity. November typically focuses on families coming together and expressing gratitude. Organizations often seek donations for those less fortunate. The contrast of a joyful Thanksgiving holiday with the homeless status of your character may be a good tie in. If you write poetry February or May may be suited to increase sales.

Most newspapers have a book review section. Typically, local freelance writers do these book reviews. You can email them with a comment on their latest book review and offer to send your book for them to read. It is important to remember that even a poor review still gets you and your book out to the public.

An example of this was an author featured on the Oprah Winfrey show, who was later found to be less than truthful in his purported memoir. The day after his appearance, his book hit the bestseller list and sales skyrocketed. Within the next few weeks as his background and his book were investigated, he continued to get more free publicity and more book sales!

A media release is not limited to newspapers. You can send them to radio stations, librarians, and to online sites that attract your target audience.

You on the Air

Radio continues to be a popular venue to educate and entertain at home, at work, and for people on the go. Many stations are on the air 24/7 and there is a constant need to fill air space with entertainment, news, current events and discussions. Talk show hosts are especially interested in published authors with books that prompt call ins from listeners. Stations are also required to offer public service announcements (PSAs), which may fall into the purview of your book.

There are specific marketing agents who make the radio contacts you need. They place your name, author information, and your 25-word pitch in their mail outs to radio stations nationwide. This may be a good opportunity, however, this service can be costly and there is no guarantee you will be contacted by a radio host for an interview.

Another option is to make direct contact with local radio stations. The advantage is that you live and work in the same community. It is often easier to talk with a host about local interests and identify needs of listeners. If the station is nearby, you may actually go to the studio and do your interviews live. Always speak and dress professionally and arrive early. Be prepared to wait, as needed, for a previous interviewee to finish or for commercial breaks.

Typically, interviews are set up via telephone and can be aired in real time or at a later date. Individuals are rarely paid for their interview time. The real pay off for you is getting your name and book out to the public. You can also mention future book fairs, book signings, or presentations where you will appear.

Some hosts will allow call-in orders for your book. You should be prepared to offer a benefit when a listener orders your book during the broadcast. This can be a discount, free postage, a gift, one book at full price, the second at half off, and similar rewards and incentives.

Here are some important points to prepare for any interview:

- Mail a copy of your book and media kit to the host ahead of time; you can also write out a list of key points or questions which he or she may want to ask.

- State your name and book title at the start and end of the interview.

- Tell listeners how they can get in touch with you for further discussion or to order your book. You may be allowed to display a table card or poster with your name, book title, email, and web address.

- Mention your education and experience, to add credibility to your discussion.

- Mention your book title at least five times. It is better if the host mentions it several times.

- Use your 25 word pitch.

- Answer questions simply; avoid technical jargon.

- During discussions and question/answer sessions, steer the listening audience back to the topic of your book.

- Prepare three major points about your book and be sure to cover them during the interview.

- Monitor the time allotted and be sure to finish on time.

- If it is a group or panel discussion, make your strongest points at the beginning of the interview.

- Never interfere with the host's agenda. Understand cues to end your remarks for a station break.

- Follow the host's lead and pattern of questions and answers.

- Thank your host while on the air.

As a professional courtesy, send the host a thank you note. Complement the host and name something specific you enjoyed. Tell him or her you are available for future on-air interviews.

Dan Poynter, popular writer of books for authors, stated three important points:

- *Writing a book is a creative activity*

- *A published book is a product*

- *Selling a book is a business*

Serious writers would benefit from these words of wisdom and should post them in a prominent place.

CHAPTER 7

Never Leave Home Without It

Consider your book to be your Siamese twin—attached at your fingertips. Always be in a position to show and tell about your book.

Keep a copy of your book in your shopping cart, brief case, car trunk, bike basket, diaper bag, pocket book, backpack, and gym bag.

Have it with you when dropping off or picking up your children, during homeowner meetings, medical appointments, at the bank, and in waiting rooms. Especially in waiting rooms. Take your book to soccer games, food shopping, church gatherings, picnics, department stores, malls, and open house night at school.

Everywhere you go, your book goes with you.

Display Copy

When you receive the first copy of your book, use it as your display copy. Place a small label on the front-bottom-right corner, stating "Display Copy."

Encourage people to pick up your book and look through it. There is something enticing about holding a book in one's hands and flipping through the pages. It may get stained or dog-eared from handling, but will also indicate many people have been interested enough to leaf through it.

This one display copy will save wear and tear on your other books. Your display copy can be used repeatedly at events, book signings, and carried with you wherever you go. Use a zip lock bag to protect it from wear and tear when not on display.

Copy Your Book Cover

Make several copies of your book cover on photo grade paper. Make various sizes for displays and posters. A quick and easy mini poster can be made by securing your book cover to a piece of cardboard (such as those on the back of legal pads) and cover it with a clear sheet protector.

Another suggestion is to create a false book cover to fit over a different book. Insert your book cover into a clear sheet protector and use it as an alias book cover to place over whatever book you are reading. Your book cover will always be on display.

P.I.T.C.H. Technique: Position In The Correct Hand

When holding your book it's beneficial for all authors to use the correct P.I.T.C.H. technique.

Your book must be strategically placed to gain attention and for optimum viewing by those passing by. Hold your book in your left hand, lean the book across your chest, angle it toward your right shoulder, front cover facing out. This is the perfect P.I.T.C.H. position and should be used when out in public. You always want your right hand free to offer a friendly hand shake when meeting people.

Now, well-versed in the P.I.T.C.H. technique, multiple business cards stuffed inside your book, and armed with your display copy (or your alias book cover) you are prepared to go forth onto the marketing trail.

As the Line Moves

I used to consider long lines a serious interruption of more important things in my life. As a published author, I now view long lines as a wonderful marketing opportunity.

Long lines are one of the few places strangers willingly strike up conversations. Usually the comments are geared toward how unnecessary the long line is. Remarks often reveal where this busy person should have been ten minutes ago, why she is in a hurry, or how this long wait is going to delay the rest of her life.

This is an opportunity for you to engage in a random act of kindness and listen attentively, commiserate with her waiting ordeal, and more importantly, steer her to your marketing department. (This also works well in waiting rooms.)

Have your book in the P.I.T.C.H. position and prepare for a typical conversation between you (Y) and the stranger (S). Here is an example you can practice.

    (S)   "I hate standing in lines."
    (Y)   "So do I. It seems to be the way things are these days."
         (offer annoyed sigh)
    (S)   "I'm in such a hurry. I could be getting so much done." (looks around at others in the line)
    (Y) "Me too. My publisher is pressuring me to finish Chapter 13 of my book."
    (S)   "You're a writer?" (asked with interest/curiosity)
    (Y)   "Yes, I am." (smile with pride)
    (S)   "Have you published a book?"
    (Y)   "Yes. The title is . . ."

At this point, you flick your wrist, shift your book downward from the P.I.T.C.H. position and place it in the empty space between you and your new-found stranger-acquaintance.

    (S)   "What's it about?" (looking at the cover)

(Y)   (Respond with your 25-word
      elevator speech)
      Pull two of your business
      cards from your book as you
      recite your 25-word pitch and
      hand them to (S)

(Y)   "Here's my book information. You
      can find (title of your book)
      in the library or you can
      order it online."

(S)   "Do they have it at such-and-
      such bookstore?"

(Y)   "I'm sure they do. You can ask
      at the service desk. They'll
      order it for you if they're
      out of stock."

(S)   "Oops. Sorry. I have two of your
      cards." (tries to hand one
      back to you)

(Y)   "That's okay. One for you and
      one for a friend." (big smile)

As the line moves, reposition your book to the P.I.T.C.H. position for better exposure. If you have spoken loudly and offered eye contact, others standing in line will have overheard your conversation and be curious about you, a real live author in their presence.

Congratulations! You've just made your début as a public speaker.

Airports

For the travelers among you, airports can be a real time waster. For the traveling author, consider it your book tour. Who's to know?

Clutching your book in the P.I.T.C.H. position, front cover facing out, move through the airport with your book proudly displayed.

Airports provide multiple opportunities for long-line conversations and one-on-one stranger conversations. Keep your book (or alias book cover) in the P.I.T.C.H. position as you approach the skycap, baggage handlers, and the security check-in line. Think about it; here you are casually conversing with the people in front of you and behind you while disrobing and baring your feet. As you fill the conveyer-belt basket with your personal items be sure your book is on top, front cover face up, of course.

Now you proceed to the clerk at the counter for check-in. Proudly keep your book in the P.I.T.C.H. position as you go through the seat-assignment-confirmation process.

While waiting, if time permits, stroll the gate area, the food court, and gift shops. Stop in the bookstore, show the clerk your book and ask if they carry it. Tell her it is so good you wanted to buy another copy for a friend.

Pull two business cards from the pages of your book. Hand one to the clerk and suggest she might be interested in reading it. Ask her to give the other card to the bookstore buyer. You want to make it as easy as possible for her to remember your request and pass along your card.

If you must sit in the waiting area, find someone with a book and sit next to her. With your book in the P.I.T.C.H. position, inquire about the book she is reading. Do your famous hand flick. Show, then tell about your book using your 25-word pitch.

Congratulations! You have just made another personal appearance. (Beware the Paparazzi!)

Real-Time Chat Rooms

I consider waiting rooms to be real—time chat rooms. Waiting rooms are full of people with time on their hands and worry in their hearts. Folks love to talk in these real-time chat rooms. Consider it another random act of kindness to engage these people in conversation. You are relieving their stress by getting their mind off their problems. Using the P.I.T.C.H. technique and the long-line strategy, you can offer your 25-words and likely have time to elaborate about you and your book. (Do not compare medications or surgery scars.)

CHAPTER 8

Coming Soon: Live and in Color

One of the most dreaded experiences for most people is public speaking. You, however, are now the survivor of several public speaking engagements: elevator pitches, long-line-stranger conversations, airport encounters, and waiting-room chats.

If the thought of a bigger audience causes you to shake, rattle, and roll, keep practicing your 25-word pitch for those single—person encounters.

As you feel more secure, start with a small group, perhaps at a private bookstore, school, library, clubhouse, church group, or book club. Invite your writing friends to come out and support you. Ask them for feedback.

A good presenter has eye contact with the audience, limits hand gestures, and moves from point to point in a clear and logical manner. He or she also monitors the level of interest and moves on when the audience seems to be bored or restless.

I Hear You

Listening is also a great strategy to promote your book. People love to find someone who will listen to them.

When you turn an understanding ear toward those who want to talk and be heard, you will pick up on key words that offer a clue to chime in about your book.

Tune in to these words: **a**uthor, **b**ook, **c**opyright, **d**edication, **e**pilogue, **f**ront page, **g**host writer, **h**ot topic, **i**ndex, **j**uvenile, **k**iddy-lit, **l**iterature, **m**oney, **n**onfiction, **o**ptions, **p**ublish, **q**uery, **r**ejection, **s**how, **t**ell, **u**nder priced, **v**alue, **w**riter, **X**-rated, **y**oung adult, **z**oom out. There are many more

key words and phrases and with
practice, you will become a pro at
finding the appropriate time to mention
your book.

Teachers are Your Friends

Schools often seek speakers to
make classroom presentations, talk at
parent meetings, or for career day.
This gives you three
possibilities. You can speak about your
day job, your work as an writer, or the
topic of your book. You can focus on
any of these aspects of your life to
make a presentation, become known as a
published author, and sell your book.

For example, you may be an
accountant (or a retired accountant,)
have published a cops-and-robbers
thriller, and enjoy fishing. Let's say
your book is titled: *Blood and Guts: A
Fish Tale of Tax Evasion and Fraud*.

Here are examples of ways to work
in your book during your presentation:

1. Your Day Job: As an accountant, I
    work with numbers, when I want to
    relax I go fishing, but my real
    love is writing. I've written a
    book (say your book title here)
    My book is about (insert your 25

words here and then elaborate.) Now tie in your love of numbers with your love of writing.

2.   About Your Book: Accounting is interesting, but not too exciting. In my spare time, I wrote a real thriller, (say your book title here). My book is about (insert your 25-words and then elaborate.) You can contrast your humdrum life as an accountant with the exciting story you wrote.

3.   You as a Fisherman: Just like fishing, an author's life can be solitary, but rewarding. It took me four years to become an accountant, three years to write my book, and two hours to catch a fish. My book, (say your book title here) is about (insert your 25-words and then elaborate.) You can compare your long hours of peaceful fishing with your long hours of solitude while writing.

To get full marketing mileage when speaking in schools, there are many ways to get you and your book remembered long after the presentation is over. Here are just a few:

- Give the teacher a free copy of your book

- Donate a book to the school media center

- If the topic of your book is appropriate for the students, you can give a copy as a door prize

- You can make work sheets for the teacher to use in conjunction with your book (vocabulary words, word searches, interesting facts, etc.)

- Provide the teacher with a media kit ahead of time including order forms for student use

- Send the teacher and students a monthly email with follow up information related to your book topic, the world of writing, or a future writer related event you plan to attend

- Offer to come back and do another presentation

- Ask the teacher for a referral to another teacher or to the media specialist

Librarians are Your Friends

In addition to books, libraries offer public service presentations. The two main benefits are: the community obtains free information and speakers have a public forum.

Using the above accountant example, you can volunteer to do a workshop on real estate tax, investing, organizing tax records, the pros and cons of online banking, or similar topics within your area of expertise. Use one of the school scenarios and work your book into your presentation.

Another excellent reason to become friends with librarians is to have them purchase your book—multiple copies if possible. As soon as your book is published, take it to the library. Give them your 25-word pitch, explain you are a local author, and ask them to order your book.

Librarians are responsive to patron requests. Ask your family, friends and neighbors to call the library and ask for your book. This technique encourages the library to make a purchase, gets more people reading your book, and keeps your book alive and well in the minds of librarians. Most libraries track request information and will order books accordingly.

Individuals often approach librarians for reading recommendations. Local book clubs and writer groups frequently use the library for monthly meetings. Contact these groups and offer to make a presentation about your book or life as a writer.

Whenever you speak to anyone about your book, always mention it is available at the library and suggest they call and request it. There are two possibilities. Either your book is in the library and will be actively circulated or it isn't yet in the library, and this will be another request for your book, which will prompt the library to purchase it.

If you ever wondered which libraries have your book, you can search online at the World Library Card Catalog. Go to www.worldcat.org and put in the title of your book and your name. A list of libraries that have your book will appear. Also included is the city, and state in the U.S. or the name of the foreign country.

Writers are Your Friends

You want your name known. You want your book to sell. You need to join a writers' group.

Writing is a solitary vocation, done in isolation. Writers come together to learn about the art and craft of good prose. They offer each other support, encouragement, and networking opportunities.

Writer's workshops and conferences can enrich your spirit and give you the boost you need to carry on during your moments of doubt.

Conferences are especially helpful for networking. Often the presenters are successful, published authors, agents, or publishing representatives.

An opportunity to pitch your book is available at most writers' conferences. You can schedule appointments with an agent or publishing representative. They offer constructive feedback and a chance for you to ask questions. If they aren't interested, they may direct you to an associate who is.

You can follow up via email with presenters to ask questions or make requests for additional information specific to your writing needs. A conference may also offer an opportunity for back-of-the-room book sales or display tables for authors to sell their books.

If there is no local writers' group, you may want to start one. Libraries and bookstores are often willing to host writers' clubs and meetings.

There are also online writers' clubs, critique groups, blogs, chat rooms, and newsletters. This level of involvement often provides leads to book reviewers, magazine articles, special interest publishers, and networking with writers.

If you find just one good idea to improve your writing, make a connection to move your book toward publication, or improve sales, it is well worth your time and money to attend book fairs, writer's workshops, and conferences.

There are national groups in specific genres which you should join for creative support and credibility as a writer. Some of the well known are:

- Academy of American Poets
- American Crime Writers League
- Mystery Writers of America
- National League of American Pen Women
- Romance Writers of America
- Science Fiction and Fantasy Writers of America
- Society of Childrens' Books Writers and Illustrators
- Western Writers of America

Other Groups and Groupies

You want to increase your list of 150 live friends by being known and connected to as many people as possible. Groups are a wonderful opportunity to share your expertise, get your name known, and pitch your book.

You need to find a group that has a common interest in something you enjoy and do well. You are an expert in something. You know more about something than most other people. Someone out there is looking for you. They want to learn what you know to make their life easier or help them become more successful.

Don't think you have anything to offer? Sure you do! Can you give advice? (think: Ann Landers.) Have you ever changed the oil in your car? (think: Click and Clack.) Have you ever done the laundry? (think: Martha Stewart.) Have you ever cooked? (think: Rachel Ray.) Have you ever had to fire someone? (think: Donald Trump.) Do you enjoy playing with computers? (think: Bill Gates.) Can you carry on a conversation? (think: Oprah.) All of these well known, rich and famous people where at one time unknown.

Groups present an opportunity for you to expand those 150 people you know and share your expertise. You can also work in a pitch for your book. You will soon become known as the group member who is a writer.

Colleges, libraries, and community centers host gatherings for card clubs, gardening, stamp collecting, local history, bird watching, and similar groups. You can also contact the local recreation department and suggest they start a group for something you are interested in, such as hair braiding, scrapbooking, pen collecting, guitar playing, or whatever excites your creative self.

There are many community service organizations and social support groups such as the Red Cross, the humane society, the Lions Club, Hospice for Humanity, community food bank, and similar organizations looking for volunteers.

Find a group where you can connect with others who have similar interests, find opportunities to make your 25-word-pitch, and gain fame as the group member or volunteer who is a published author.

Book Signings

Book signings are a wonderful opportunity for readers to meet authors. Many readers have private library collections, belong to book clubs, or do book trading. They often purchase autographed books as gifts.

Keep in mind book signings do not have to take place only in bookstores. Cafes, health food stores, and gift shops, are just a few alternatives for book signings. If you have a specialty book, for example, on sky diving, a sporting goods store might be eager to offer you a book display and book signing.

Book signings are usually arranged directly with the bookstore manager. Larger chain stores may have an individual who handles community events such as this. With independently owned bookstores, you may be dealing directly with the owner or store manager. These people are highly vested in your success as an author and your ability to draw people into their bookstore.

Available inventory is another important factor. Most bookstores will not allow you to sell your own books directly to the customer. You must be sure the bookstore has placed a book order in a timely manner with the distributor to have enough books for sale at your book signing.

Often the bookstore will advertise your book signing with a flier or news release. You should also make your own fliers to give to friends, family, neighbors, and members of your interest group. You can send out a press release announcing your upcoming book signing. Newspapers seek information about local authors and events for their weekly calendars, so be sure they have your book signing information.

A book signing is a full commitment of time. Arrive about an hour early, plan to be there for several hours, and stay after to network and pack up.

Wear comfortable clothes and shoes. If you have a costume, outfit, or T-Shirt that ties in with your book, it will draw more attention. If you have give-a-away items that relate to your story, be sure to clear it with the bookstore sponsor. Have a plentiful supply of your promotional materials, including your business cards, and order forms. Also, collect email addresses for future contact.

There are many variables involved in book signings. Timing alone is a critical element: time of day, day of the week, and season of year all make a difference. The size and location of the store will determine the number and type of shoppers you can expect. Is it a stand-alone store, one of many in a mall, or one of four shops in a strip plaza? Is it a private bookstore or part of a chain? Was there publicity? Were there promotional events?

Location of your presentation inside the store-near the front door, in the café, or at the children's table —is also important.

Many authors have successful book signings with plentiful sales and are asked to come again. Other authors have few sales and are so disappointed they consider it a lot of work, a waste of time, and of little benefit.

As with any effort to market your book, consider a book signing a promotional opportunity. Meet and talk with as many people as possible, especially the employees. Strike up your P.I.T.C.H. pose and smile at all customers.

Be prepared for no one to show up, or to be overrun with a crowd of eager buyers!

Book Fairs

One of the easiest and least expensive endeavors for authors is a book fair. There are major book fairs, with hundreds of exhibitors or smaller local book fairs with a limited number of authors. You must consider time, travel, and expenses when deciding which type of book fair will best suit your needs.

The benefits of attending a book fair cannot be overstated. It is a marketing opportunity with direct and indirect rewards.

A book fair will help reawaken your muse as you mix and mingle with other writers. The book fair publicity typically contains your name, book title, and contact information. Fliers will be given out to visitors and participants with this information.

Additionally, you will gain:

- Individual publicity for you and your work

- Networking opportunities with other professionals in your field

- An opportunity to sign and sell your books

- Access to speaker presentations

- A list of names, email addresses, and book titles of other participants for future networking

- Opportunity to view and discuss marketing ideas with other authors

Often, you walk away with a gift basket, door prize, professional name tag, table sign, or poster.

CHAPTER 9

Your Other Writing

Writing has many venues. You can practice your writing skills and help others at the same time. Of course, you always want your name, book title, and bio at the end of everything you write.

You the Helper

You can write or edit a notice for your church bulletin, homeowner newsletter, or recreation department. You can write helpful hints and post them on bulletin boards in your community, supermarket, or your child's school.

You might offer tips on other uses for vinegar, how to get gum out of a toddler's hair, how to entice your cat to try new food, how to put your dog on a diet, or how to replant rose bushes. You can write about common tasks that you have found a faster, easier, or less costly way of doing.

These little tidbits of writing will give you name recognition as an author and build your confidence in networking with others.

You the Expert

You are an expert in something—remember? You can easily write an article about something you understand and do well.

A simple piece of 500 to 1000 words can be sent to a specialty magazine and carry your name in the by-line and your book title in the bio at the end of the article. There are free publications supported by advertising, trade publications, and those devoted to hobbies. They may look like newsletters, small newspapers, or thick brochures.

The majority of material comes from freelance writers. Depending on the frequency of publication, editors often need 20 or more pieces each week or month. They are always looking for new articles. These magazines may focus on real estate, parenting, sports, small town living, unusual occupations, fitness after 50, woodworking projects, the at-home worker, cake decorating, holiday entertaining, dating for the workaholic, and so on.

The most popular type of articles for specialty magazines are the "How-to", the "Round-up," and the "Evergreen."

The How-to Article

These articles begin with a two or three sentence introduction and end in a similar fashion with a short summary. The body of the article offers bulleted tips or suggestions for the interested reader. The more specific the information the more appealing it will be and the more likely to be published. Consider these intriguing possibilities:

Seven Easy Steps To...
- Learn bird calls
- Earn money with your computer

- Fashion design success
- Stop a leaky faucet
- Bake pies on a BBQ grill
- Tame your pet monkey
- Double your income
- Change careers after 40

In addition to the title and your name, the how-to piece typically has the following sections: a brief introductory paragraph about your topic, a list of tips or steps to complete a task, and a summary paragraph at the end. Then comes the most important part: your biography. The bio includes your name and a few sentences with some personal information. This is where you can put the name of your book, and your contact information.

Here is an example of a "How-to" article. If you are a parent, a nurse or worked in a medical setting, you could write an article about toddler safety at home. Make your article as specific as possible. Your title may be *Five Steps for a Safer Medicine Cabinet.*

Your introductory paragraph would include general information about the type of items found in most home medicine cabinets, the high risk for children who gain access to solvents and medications, and statistics about children who have died or been injured after exploring the medicine cabinet.

The body of the article is a list of safety tips for parents to protect their children from the dangerous contents of home medicine cabinets. These are usually one or two sentences of general, practical suggestions, listed as bulleted text.

Your last paragraph should offer a summary of the dangers and focus on the actions parents can take to prevent injury and increase safety.

The Round-up Article

The Round-up piece compares and contrasts. For example, you may list five Mexican Restaurants in your area and compare the cost, menu items, location, and service at each. You can do this with child-care centers, bowling allies, movies, dry cleaners, banks, office supply stores, health foods, and so on. Typically, four to six points are compared for each, giving both advantages and disadvantages. The most important part of your article is your bio at the end with your name and book titles.

Evergreens

Evergreens are standard articles, that coincide with events and holidays throughout the year. Magazine editors are constantly on the watch for these gems to show up for their review and publication.

Typical titles might be: *Life Long Valentines: Fifty Years of Marriage*, *Six Tips for Super Birthday Parties*, *Cool Fun in the July Sun*, or *Overcoming Stress During the Holidays*.

Whether a "How-to," a "Round-up," or an "Evergreen," most magazines have a payment range from $20.00 to $50.00, usually based on word count. The advantage is you can sell these articles again as reprints, continue to make money, and get exposure for your other writing. This is a nice reward for your time and adds to your credibility as a writer, but your goal is free advertising for you and your book. Your real payoff is in your bio at the end of the article.

It's up to you to write your bio and place it at the end of your article. Keep it less than 50 words, put in something of interest to the reader, your email address, and your book title.

108

CHAPTER 10

Hard Copy

Hard copy is alive and well. Delivered in a written format, hard copy allows individuals to process information at their convenience, on their time line, in their comfort zone.

Despite the joys of e-world communication and videos, people still like to have and hold something permanent in their hands. They want to sit and read at their leisure. They like the look and feel of hard copy materials. People like to sit in their favorite chair, on the porch swing, the patio chaise lounge, the picnic table, or at the beach and read.

They want to educate themselves and inform others. They like to pass along a book, a magazine, a newspaper clipping, business card, or informational flier about a product or service. Hard copy serves as a reminder, a reference, and as a springboard for conversation with others.

Hard copy is mixed media. It affords you the opportunity to display your work in text and pictures. Whether you design and print your own materials, or use a hired professional, you need to generate design ideas. Start to collect fliers and see which ones grab your attention. Look for a pattern of colors, format, text, graphics, and design which you find pleasing, attract your attention, and covey the most information. The text and graphics you select should lead the reader into your book, peak their curiosity, and get them to want more.

When creating text for your hard copy materials keep in mind, the word that attracts most readers is the word *you*. Research in the area of direct mail has uncovered a list of power words that draw the most attention and increase sales. Try to use as many of these twelve power words as possible when writing about you and your book.

- Discover
- Easy
- Guarantee
- Health
- Love
- Money
- New
- Proven
- Safety
- Save
- Results
- You

Fliers and Brochures

The purpose of a flier or brochure is to get your name and book out to others and provide ordering information.

A flier is an inexpensive promotional tool, which you can make on a computer and have copied at a local print shop. It can be used as a mailer, placed in display racks, given directly to individuals or groups, used as part of a media kit, or as a press release.

A full-page flier can have your basic information at the top and ordering information at the bottom. You can use the back of the flier to print the first page of your book to invite reader's interest.

A half page flier can have your basic information on the left side and ordering information on the right. Be sure to use the back of the flier for added information such as a presentation you've made, an upcoming workshop, or a book signing. This is also a good place for reviews of your book, awards you've received, or bookstores and book clubs that carry your book. You can use the back of the flier for inspirational quotes, the tag line from your book, events that have to do with your book's content and so on.

Minimal basic information for your flier includes:

- Book cover
- Book title
- Your name
- Your 25 words
- Contact information

You should also include a call to action. Tell the potential reader to buy your book! You can offer special benefits such as:

- 10% discount if purchased by a certain date
- Gift with each purchase
- Free bonus book with multi-book orders
- Free postage

Provide as many options as possible to order your book. Typically, books can be ordered from the publisher, the author, bookstores, book clubs, and online booksellers. If your book is also available in specialty shops or locations, such as a pet center, museum, hospital gift shop, college library, and so on, be sure to indicate that as well.

Include an order form for direct purchase from you with the added benefit of receiving an autographed copy of your book. Along with their mailing address, request their email address to add to your ever-growing online contact list.

If they order via email, be sure to respond and let them know you've received their order, tell when the book was mailed, and thank them for their support. This is a good time to make one of those special offers. You can make future sales by offering a discount or free shipping on their next order.

To keep track of your marketing efforts, put an alphanumeric code on the order form. Embed the month and year into the code. You can also use letters to indicate where you placed your flier, for example, "LB" for library, "SL" for school, "BF" for book fair, "WG" for writers' group, "CS" for coffee shop, or "BB" for bulletin board. Your code may look something like this 092012-BF Some authors use different color fliers each month to track high and low sale cycles.

Always print across the bottom or use a footer to state, "Copies of this form are acceptable." This will encourage people to keep your flier intact, and, hopefully, pass it along to a friend.

Newsletters

Newsletters can be created inexpensively on your computer, and sent via email or printed and copied at your local print shop. Put a copy of your newsletter inside every book you sell.

For a newsletter to be effective, you must be consistent in mailing or distributing it at regular intervals. The newsletter carries your basic

information, book titles, and ordering
details. More than half of the
newsletter should be devoted to
informative articles, helpful hints,
interesting facts, and new ideas for
your reader. Make your newsletter
interactive in some way to invite your
readers to be involved. You can have a
quiz or a contest. The prize can be an
offer of a free one-time mention of
their book or business in the next
issue. You can make this same offer if
they contact you with a tip,
information, or feedback.

A novel that focuses on a theme
such as science fiction, medical drama,
family relationships, or military
events, may also benefit from a
marketing newsletter. Aside from
promoting you and your book, it could
include the latest happenings in that
venue, such as artificial intelligence,
stem-cell research, Grandparents Day,
or facts about U.S. military academies.

Post Cards

Post cards are a multipurpose
direct mail piece. To be cost effective
and reach your intended book buyer,
there are several basic rules to
follow. Some research has indicated

individuals have to see something six times before they take notice and act on the content or message. This demonstrates the need for mail outs at regular intervals.

Post cards come in all sizes and shapes. To pay a lower postage rate, size your post card within the United States Postal Service regulations. A basic rectangle shape is best for display and ease of handling.

The face of the post card should be the cover of your book, showing the title and your name. A book cover that is clear, crisp, with bright colors will work best for post cards. Avoid muted colors or background printing when designing your book cover. This type of cover does not copy well, and is difficult to use for post cards, posters, and related promotional materials.

The reverse of the post card is configured into two sections. On the right half, you will have two items. The postage stamp in the far right upper corner and in the left upper section is your name, book title, and return address. Always use a post office box as your return address, never your actual physical home address. There are many strange people in the world and you do not want one of them showing up for a surprise visit. The mid section of the right side is blank for the mailing label or address.

The back left of the reverse side of the post card should contain the following information:

- Your name
- Title of the book(s)
- Your 25 words
- Your tag line
- ISBN and cost
- How to order
- A link to your web page
- Your email address
- Call to action

Leave at least a ¼ inch margin on all sides of the post card for the postal barcode and other markings.

Ordering should be as simple as possible. Offer various options for ordering your book: direct from the author, the publisher, online booksellers, bookstores, or book clubs. Also, suggest they contact the library. If enough people request your book, the library will purchase it.

The call to action tells the potential buyer what to do and what they will get in return. This is similar to your special offers. Here are some examples:

- *Purchase directly from the author for an autographed copy.*

- *Return this post card with your order and receive an autographed copy, 10% discount, and free postage!*

- *Order within the next 10 days and get a second book at half price.*

- *Order 10 books and get one free.*

Post cards can be made by a local printer or ordered online through large specialized promotional companies. Typically, the higher the number of post cards you order, the lower the unit price. In addition to the actual postcard, costs also include postage (second-class stamp), a mailing label, and your time.

Many post cards will be returned to you with a wrong address or an expired forwarding order. Use these to update your database mailing list, correcting and purging information. You can also be creative and make use of these returned post cards in a variety of ways, including:

- Cover the old label and use them as samples at writers' workshops, conferences, and meetings

- Use them to make false book covers

- Paste them onto construction paper, make mini posters, and note cards

- Make wall hangings by pasting the post card to the upper part of poster board and on the bottom, use calligraphy to write something inspirational or the tag line from your book and give them as gifts

Mailing Lists

When using direct mail you want to target your potential readers and buyers. You can purchase mailing lists or create your own database.

Purchasing a mailing list will save you time. The down side is cost. Another problem is that it may not have been updated recently, increasing the return rate and postage costs. Usually, these lists are purchased for one-time use only.

Making your own database takes computer skills and is time consuming. You can, however, have a better-targeted list, which you can update continuously and use over and over. You can find lists of local, state, and national organizations for your targeted audience.

For example, this book, *Write, Publish, Sell!* is specifically targeted to those interested in writing, publishing, marketing, and selling their books. Good sources to create my database are other writers, agents, and publishers. Each time I attend a writer's group, workshop, or convention I collect business cards with names, addresses and emails. This information is often easily found in books and online web pages or blogs of authors and writers' groups. Writer's magazines are filled with information about services for writers, including editing, ghost writing, copywriters, and so on, most with mailing and email information. All of these provide information to continuously build and update my current mailing list.

CHAPTER 11

The Online Confuser

If you break out in a rash at the mention of the word *computer*, take heart. There are quick and easy ways to use your computer for marketing you and your work without needing a Ph.D. in computer science. Everyone who has ever used a computer knows when they work, they are wonderful, and when they don't work, they are not.

E-Mail Signature

At the very minimum, you should have an email address. You should create a specific email address for your writing. Your can use your name with the word *Writer*, or *Author*, or *Books*. Many email names are already in use, so you may have to be creative. For example my email address is VAllenWriter@cs.com. This is used for online communication and as a promotional tool. Most people have more than one email address. They keep one for personal email and another for emails related to their writing.

An easy promotional tool is to add a permanent signature line that will appear on every email you send. Your signature line should contain your name and book title(s). You can be more elaborate and include the ISBN, and a link to your web page, as well. If you have online profiles, you may want to have these in your email signature. The point is to offer contact information every time you send out an email.

Weave a Web Page

More and more authors use a web page to offer detailed information about themselves and their book(s). They can also sell other products and services and link to other web sites for writers. You can have excerpts from your books, offer writing tips, or have a list of books helpful to authors.

Some web pages are free with your email browser, others you have to pay for. If you have computer skills, you may be able to make a web site using a template or create your own. You will have to register a domain name for your web page. Again, try to use your name and the words, *author* or *writer*. My web page is www.ValerieAllenWriter.com.

If it is a one-page web site, organize your information from most important to least important. People move quickly when viewing a web page, so you want to have the most important information at the top of the page.

Start with your book title(s) and your name. With only those two facts, someone who wanted your book could find it and place an order. List other information such as the ISBN, the publisher, your 25 words, information about the author and so on down the page.

If you have a multi-page site, make it easy to navigate from page to page. This is done by the use of radio buttons or tabs. Each page should also have a quick way to return to the home page. There should be plenty of 'white space' on each page. You do not need to cram every inch of space on your web pages. Keep it uncluttered, and easy to understand. Be sure to include your email address, web page address, and any online profile addresses on each page. You can do this with a footer across the bottom.

An example of a five-page web site may include a page for each of these topics:

- Home Page with your contact information
- My Book Page with your book cover(s), your 25 words, and a story summary. Also list awards or upcoming book signings, presentations and so on
- Information for readers and tips for writers
- Ordering information
- About the author

Blogs

Web logs, or blogs for short, are a great way to get you and your book out there. You can find blogs dedicated specifically to writers. You can also find blogs that appeal to your target readers, those interested in you or your book topic. You can ask questions, offer feedback, enter a discussion and so on. The important thing is your signature bio at the end of your blog. Just as with your email signature line, you want your name and book title to appear.

Another blogging opportunity is to offer to do a guest post on someone else's blog site. This will put your name out there in the writing world. If you do this consistently, you may find yourself in demand as an online writer. As a guest blogger, you won't have the demand of coming up with new content and you can offer blogs as time allows in your writing schedule.

You can easily create your own blog with online systems that are free and offer templates. Blogs are time consuming. If you decide to have your own blog, you must continuously have new content. You must also have a consistent method of marketing your blog site so people will find it online. You must attract readers to your blog with articles of interest, writing tips, or free offers.

Online Bookstores

Clicks count. Find your book at online booksellers and click on the cover to open the page dedicated to your book. When not at home, ask others if you can use their computer to check your book online. The more clicks from different computers the higher your ranking. You will also gain attention as others to go online, look at your book and click the like button near the top of the page.

At least once a week, go to online booksellers and make sure your book is still there. See if anyone has added a review of your book. See if any other author has referenced your book in his or her book. Find out which books people bought after they purchased your book. You can go to the web page of these authors and send them an email based on the similarity of your books.

Most online booksellers offer a free author profile page, a book shelf to show your books, and lists for you to showcase your favorite books. You can also do book reviews for other authors. Every time you read or listen to a book, you should take the time to offer a review.

You can become a book reviewer for online bookstores. After you read a book, find it at an online bookstore, give it a ranking and write a review. You will have an opportunity to use a signature line, which can include your name and the name of your book. As your name shows up repeatedly with these book reviews, it will encourage people to find your book online, visit your web page or send you an email.

These book reviews are helpful to the author and your name will be displayed as the reviewer. This is a good investment of your time to lead people to you, your book(s), and your profile, which in turn will encourage them to view your web page and books.

When I review a book online, I give it a four or five star rating. I can safely and truthfully say this, because if I couldn't offer a high rating, I would not do the online book review. In that case, I try to contact the author directly and offer my opinions privately rather than have a public negative review. After all, the review is just my opinion and I am trying to support another author.

Media Book Reviews

You can easily peruse the online editions of large newspapers and see if they do book reviews. You can email them and request a review of your book. Typically, you will mail them your media kit and ask them to contact you if and when your review is posted.

Have friends, family members and co-workers read your book and send you an email with their feedback. You can use their comments for quotes about your book on the back cover, on hard copy materials, or book displays.

The newspaper may also feature a story or article about someone who has a unique interest in the topic of your book. You can contact him or her, offer to send them a free book and request their comments and feedback. If they were favorable, this would provide you with credibility as well as a good quote to use. You have also connected with one more person (and his or her 150 people) with an interest in your topic.

You can also get good press by offering your support to groups or community agencies. If your book has a theme, you can tie it into a worthy cause and donate your book as a door prize for a fund raiser. Sometimes this results in a write up of the event and your name and book are mentioned as a donor. Some agencies print a flier with the names of donors and offer a special thank you. They may offer you a free ticket to their event or invite you to speak at some future date.

Google Alert

Google has a function to alert you when topics related to your book appear online or in hard copy. You provide the key words and Google does a daily search and emails you the results. You can read the articles, keep up to date in your field of interest and obtain a contact for a book review or an interview. You can also list your book free on Google.com.

Social Media

There are many online social networking groups. These present unlimited possibilities for marketing your book and connecting with others in the field.

You must first decide on your goal for joining a social networking group. Do you want to make true friends online? Do you just want to focus on furthering your writing career?

If you are seeking true friendship, this would mean the same responsibilities as with live, real-time friends. It's the give and take of conversation, being available for them, responding to them, caring about the ups and downs of their every day life.

Perhaps, you want to use your online networking strictly to promote your writing. This would present a different approach. You would join social group of writers and authors. You would share tips and information related to writing, publishing, and marketing. You would ask questions and post responses to the comments and inquiries of others. It would be an opportunity to mention the launch of your new book, an award, or book signing. It will lead you to writers' blogs where you can offer to do a guest post. It will expose you to their books.

The possibilities for using your computer and online communication to promote you and your book are endless. The only limitation is time.

APPENDIX 1

Commonly Used Abbreviations

ABA   = American Booksellers Association
ABI   = Advanced book information
ALA   = American Library Association
APA   = American Psychological Association
            (Writing Style)
APR   = Advanced print run
ARC   = Advanced review copy
BOR   = Back of the room sales
CIP   = Cataloging in publication record
CMS   = Chicago Manual of Style
DBA   = Doing business as
EAN   = Bar code for books
EM   = End matter
F & G   = Folded and gathered signature pages of a
            book
CMYK   = Four basic colors: (C) cyan; (M) magenta;
            (Y) yellow; (K) black
CE   = Copy editor
DPI   = Dots per inch
FAQ   = Frequently asked questions
FN   = Footnote
HTML   = Hypertext markup language
IPPY   = Independent Publishers Book Awards
ISBN   = International Standard Book Number
ISSN   = International Standard Serial Number
KLT   = Kate L. Turabian (Writing Style)

LCCN	=	Library of Congress Catalog Card Number
MLA	=	Modern Language Association of America (Writing Style)
NAIP	=	National Association of Independent Publishers
OCR	=	Optical character recognition scanning
OOP	=	Out of print
PMA	=	Publishers' Marketing Association
POD	=	Print on demand
POP	=	Point of purchase
PR	=	Public relations
Q & A	=	Questions and Answers
RFQ	=	Request for quote
ROI	=	Return on investment
SAN	=	Standard Address Number
SASE	=	Self addressed stamped envelope
SCBWI	=	Society of Childrens' Book Writers and Illustrators
SPAN	=	Small Publishers Association of North America
SPAWN	=	Small Publishers, Artists, and Writers Network
TIFF	=	Tagged image file format
VBT	=	Virtual book tour

APPENDIX 2

Books for Every Writers' Shelf

1,001 Ways to Market Your Books, John Kremer,
    Open Horizons

1,818 Ways to Write Better & Get Published,
    Scott Edelstein, Writer's Digest Books

A Man of My Words, Richard Lederer, St. Martin's Press

Bird by Bird, Anne Lamott, Anchor/Doubleday Books

Class Act: Sell More Books Through School & Library Author
Appearances, Barbara Techel, Joyful Paw Prints Press, LLC

Creative Juice, Terra Pressler, Ph.D., Disc-Us Books, Inc.

Eating an Elephant, Write Your Life One Bite at a Time,
    Patricia Charpentier

Getting Your Manuscript Sold C. L. Sterling &
    M. G. Davidson, Barclay House

Hooking the Reader: Opening Lines that Sell,
    Sharon Rendell-Smock, Morris Pub.

How to Write a Book Proposal, Michael Larsen,
    Writer's Digest Books

How to Write a Book and Get it Published, David Strode
    Akens, Edorts Publishing

How to Write Short Stories, Sharon Sorenson, Simon &
        Schuster Macmillan

Insider's Guide to Getting an Agent, Lori Perkins,
        Writer's Digest Books

Make That Scene, William Noble, Eriksson Publishers

Make Your Words Work, Gary Provost, Writer's Digest
        Books

Mosquito Marketing for Authors, Michelle Dunn,
        Never Dunn Publishing LLC

On Writing, Stephen King, Pocket Books

On Writing Well, William Zinsser, Perennial/Harper &
        Row

Practical Short Story Writing, John Paxton Sheriff,
        Barnes & Noble

Relaxing the Writer, Amber Polo, Wordshaping Press

Revising Fiction A Handbook for Writers, David Madden,
        Barnes & Noble

Smarter Branding Without Breaking the Bank,
        Brenda Bence, Gloal Insight Communications

Starting from Scratch, Rita Mae Brown, Bantam

The Art & Craft of Novel Writing, Oakley Hall, Story Press

The Art of Creative Writing, Lajos Egri, Citadel Press

The Elements of Style, Strunk and White

*The End: Closing Lines of Theatrically Released American
    Films,* R. Donna Chesher

The Frugal Book Promoter Carolyn Howard-Johnson,
    CreateSpace

The Frugal Editor, Carolyn Howard-Johnson,
    Red Engine Press

The Great Grammar Book Marsha Sramek

The Weekend Novelist, Robert J. Ray, Bantam Doubleday
    Dell Publishing Group

*Word Magic for Writer*s,Cindy Rodgers, Writers' Institute
    Publication

Writing Content: Mastering Magazine and Online Writing,
    Roger W. Nielsen, R. W Nielsen & Company

Writing Down the Bones, Natalie Goldberg, Shambhala

Writing for Children, Catherine Woolley (Jane Thayer),
    Penguin

APPENDIX 3

Writing for Children

Categories of Children's Books

Although they may differ slightly from publisher to publisher, there are six basic categories of children's books, including:

1. *Board Books and Picture Books* are for infants through preschool up to about the age five. The books have few pages, often one or two words per page and large colorful illustrations. They may be concept books such as learning colors, shapes and numbers. These books are also used to introduce or reinforce nouns such as apple, boat, cat, dog, elephant, or verbs such as catch, drink, eat, jump, run, etc. The focus is on the illustrations to tell a simple story or teach a concept.

2. *Read-To-Me Stories* are typically for children from preschool through second grade, ages four to seven. An adult reads to the child. Illustrations carry a simple story or present concepts in a new style, such as learning numbers while at the supermarket or naming animals during a visit to the zoo.

3. *Easy Reader/Chap Books* are for children in first through third grade, ages five to eight. Children are in the beginning reader stage, sometimes referred to as emergent readers. These books can have up to 40 pages and provide a simple story or learning concept. Stories often relate to social issues, such as friendship, truth, fairness, responsibility, and similar values. They typically focus on common events in a child's life, such as a visit to the dentist, a new baby at home, or a lost toy. These stories have a clear message and a happy ending without ambiguity.

4. *Chapter Books* are for grades two through five, ages eight to twelve. They may have between 80 to 150 pages and can be fiction or nonfiction. Fiction becomes more complex with several characters and multiple problems for the child to deal with. It's critical to have the child, as the main character, resolve the conflicts and attain his goal or meet his needs with minimal adult involvement. Non-series books appeal to this age group and include historical, science fiction, fantasy, and action adventure stories with a clear-cut story, a feeling of satisfaction for a lesson learned, and a happy ending.

5. *Series Books.* are for sixth through ninth grades, ages 10 to 14. The same main character and her friends or siblings have various adventures from book to book. Two of the most popular of these series books are *Nancy Drew* and *The Hardy Boys.*

More recent series books are the *Boxcar Children*, *Lemony Snicket*, and the *American Girls.*

6. *Young Adult (YA)* are popular with mature middle grade and high school students, ages 14 to 18. These books, fiction or nonfiction, often focus on coming-of-age issues, independence vs. family values, romance/first love, peer conflicts, good vs. evil, and global social issues such as war, hunger, or the economy. YA is often reality based and may manifest negative concepts and destructive worldviews, as well as feel-good endings of success and satisfaction for the main character.

Write, Publish, Sell!　　　　　　　　　*Valerie Allen*

Take Aim and Target

Your Children's Writing

Nowhere is it more important to target your readers than when you write for children. Children's writers must keep in mind four basic considerations: the child's age, grade, reading level, and interests to successfully reach their target audience.

Age Level

Most children enjoy reading about characters who are older than they are. Children want to reach beyond their peers and experience possible future events in the here and now. Most children's books are written within an age range, for example, 6 to 9 years or 10 to 12 years.

Grade Level

Grade level is usually an indication of a child's reading skills. Books do not have to be written at an exact grade level, but again, within a grade range, such as preschool through Kindergarten, or sixth through eighth grades.

Most computers can easily provide the reading level by grade. This is often written as 3.2 meaning third grade second month or 7.9, which means seventh grade ninth month. Keep in mind grade levels are based on the school year with September as the first month. A reading level of 4.5 would indicate the youngster is in January of the fourth grade.

Reading Level
There are 250 basic sight words, which make up approximately 70% of all reading. Most children have mastered these words by the end of third grade. Basic sight words are typically one, two, or three letter words. An informal way to check your sight words is to highlight all of the little words on a given page of writing.

Interests
Books based on hobbies and interests are varied and must be written within the youngster's age and grade level. Vocabulary is critical in these books and the author often includes an index of terms and definitions, with or without diagrams. Both fiction and nonfiction can be used to engage a child in reading about his or her hobby or interest. Using the solar system as an example, you could write a book that:

1. Describes the solar system and encourages learning and understanding

2. Provides facts, greatest moments or important figures in space exploration

3. Tells a story involving a child who wants to walk on the moon

APPPENDIX 4: Tips for Writers

Good Sentences: Word by Word

Sentences group words together to make a complete thought. Words should sound natural and flow smoothly from one point to the next. A sentence must provide information and move a story forward without confusion.

A basic sentence has a subject and a predicate, sometimes called the noun-verb pattern. The subject contains a noun and tells who or what is doing something. The predicate contains the verb which is the action word. Strong sentences follow the subject -predicate pattern.

More complex sentences may include:

- Modifiers – adjectives and adverbs

- Clauses – a group of words within the sentence that have both a subject and a predicate and make a complete thought

- Phrases – a group of words without both a subject and predicate, that adds details, but does not make a complete thought

An effective sentence has six aspects:

1. Good composing:
   Here is an alligator.

2. Appropriate punctuation:
   George, the alligator, attacked me.
   George, the alligator attacked me!

3. Feeling for the rhythm of language:
   I dared to dance and felt the music lift my soul.

4. Understanding of idioms: an expression which means something different from what the words actually state.
   It's raining cats and dogs.

5. Clarity of expression:
   There was a heavy rainstorm.
   The rain beat against the windows.

6. Power of logical arrangement
   When he opened the doors, his eyes flew across the room, and then he slammed them shut. (confusing)

   When he opened the doors, his eyes scanned the room, and then he slammed the doors shut. (improved)

Mighty Monosyllables

We are told to write tight is to write well. Do not use three words when one will do. Use one strong verb to get the job done.

The above paragraph is an example of using one-syllable words to convey exact meaning. English has many powerful one-syllable words, 20 of which make up approximately 25% of all spoken English. In order of frequency, the most often used one-syllable words are:

1. I
2. You
3. The
4. A
5. To
6. Is
7. It
8. That
9. Of
10. And
11. In
12. What
13. He
14. This
15. Have
16. Do
17. She
18. Not
19. On
20. They

Use the *find* feature on your computer to see how many times you have used these mighty monosyllabic words for tighter writing.

Ol' Whatshisname!

When naming your characters it's tempting to give your friends, family, coworkers and others a chance at their 15 minutes of fame in your story. Before indulging in the name game consider the following:

1. Names have many implications such as: status, education, religion, and place of birth

2. Short names with hard sounds such as Max, Kurt, Nick, Zena are often used for the bad guys (or gals)

3. Two syllable names are typically used for children or to portray child like qualities: Bobby, Cathy, Jimmy, Lulu

4. Single, multiple names and initials imply importance: Cher, Madonna, John Philip Sousa, Frank Lloyd Wright, JFK, FDR, MLK

5. Names indicate ethnicity: Maria, Juan, Eileen, Anthony, Lisa, Spiro, Vijay

6. The spelling of a name can reveal age and/or character traits: Smith vs. Smyth, Elizabeth vs. Lizabeth, Rose Ann vs. Rosanne

7. Names must fit the theme or time period of your story: biblical, Civil War era, Franklin or Eleanor, Shirley (Temple), Douglas (MacArthur), Chelsea (Clinton)

147

8. Nicknames are used for extroverted characters: Barb, Liz, Bill, Joe, Rick. They can also be used to reveal characterization: Shorty, Babe, Honey, Slim, Hot Stuff, Junior

9. Rule of thumb is only one common name (Jim Jones) and only one exotic name (Theodora Tinasia Peacock) per story

10. Use unique names for each character, not: Jack and Jake nor Mary and Marla

11. Last names follow the same rule, do not have: Jamison, Johnson, Jenson, Jepson

12. Names can have special meanings: grandfather/father/son, Sr, Jr. The III, use of family names as a first name (Fulbright, Hathaway) unisex names (Taylor, Parker, Madison), flowers (Rose, Buttercup, Lily), gems (Ruby, Pearl), nature (Summer, River, Plum)

Readers make an association with names based on their unique experiences, however, stereotyping is alive and well. What does Bertha look like inside your head?

Pesky Pronouns

Use a pronoun in place of a noun. An antecedent is the noun that a pronoun replaces. All pronouns must agree with their antecedent in number, person, and gender.

Various types of pronouns and examples include: personal (I), relative (who), demonstrative (that), interrogative (which), intensive (himself), reflexive (themselves) and indefinite (anybody).

Personal pronouns are used most often and tell us whether the pronoun is speaking, being spoken to, or being spoken about. Pronouns can be singular, plural or stand-alone.

Here are examples of personal pronouns:

- Subject singular: I, you, he, she, it

- Subject plural: we, you, they

- Object singular: me, you, him, her, it

- Object plural: us, you, them

- Possessive before a noun: my, your, his, her, its, our, their

- Stand alone: mine, yours, his, hers, its, ours, theirs

To avoid ambiguity in pronoun use, be aware of antecedent agreement and pronoun shift.

Examples of correct usage:

- <u>Valerie</u> doesn't like spinach, but <u>she</u> likes peas. (subject/singular)

- <u>Lee and Andy</u> said <u>they</u> were going swimming. (subject/plural)

- <u>Judy</u> didn't have a good time at <u>her</u> party.(object singular)

- <u>Frank and Mike </u> said the book belonged to<u> them.</u> (object/plural)

- The <u>boys</u> feared the steep hill, but <u>their</u> courage prevailed.(possessive)

- This cat is <u>mine</u>. (stand alone)

Pronouns can be tricky when they shift in a sentence, are placed too far away from the antecedent or are not clearly used to replace a specific noun.

Repetitive Redundancies

Redundancy: needlessly repetitive

In an effort to clarify meaning, writers often add extra words. However, the effort to explain often results in redundancy. Remember, the fewer words used to convey information the greater the impact.

Here are some sneaky repeat offenders to watch for in your writing:
- He presented <u>true</u> facts at the trial.
- They were <u>completely</u> surrounded on all sides.
- He shrugged <u>his shoulders</u>.
- He nodded <u>his head</u> <u>up and down</u>.
- She shook her head <u>from side to side</u>.
- The skunk was in close proximity <u>to my</u> <u>immediate vicinity</u>.
- It was a<u>n unexpected</u> surprise.
- Allow me to reiterate <u>what I have said before</u>.
- He found a <u>quick</u> short cut to the park.
- Please proceed <u>ahead</u>.
- He designed a <u>new</u> innovation.
- He was killed <u>dead</u>.
- They offered a <u>free</u> gift.
- He told the <u>honest</u> truth.
- One can learn from <u>past</u> experience and <u>past</u> history.
- After you have read this, I ask those guilty of using redundancies to please stand <u>up</u>.

Sentence No Nos

Good writing not only exemplifies what we should do, but what we should not do. There are specific writing *no-nos,* which preclude a well-written story.

FANBOYS: for; and; nor; but; or; yet; so
    FANBOYS are seven small words used as coordinators within a sentence. Although sometimes used effectively in the hands of skilled writers, avoid *FANBOYS* to begin a sentence. *FANBOYS* show no action and lead to wordiness. For example:

- <u>For</u> one long moment, I stood still.
- I stood still for one long moment.

- <u>And</u> I asked her what she really meant.
- I asked her what she really meant.

- <u>Nor</u> will I ever do that again.
- I will never do that again.

- <u>But,</u> I won't take no for an answer.
- I won't take no for an answer.

- <u>Or,</u> you could drop me off first, and then go fishing.
- You could drop me off first, and then go fishing.

- <u>Yet,</u> he still didn't seem to understand the message.
- He still didn't seem to understand the message.

- <u>So,</u> I went to my room and cried myself to sleep.

- I went to my room and cried myself to sleep.

Weak Verbs

A strong sentence lies in the power of strong verbs. Active verbs help the reader visualize movement such as: bump, catch, etch, jump, run, saunter, etc. Avoid the passive *to be* verbs: am, are, is, was, were. These *to be* verbs are overused, show no action, lead to wordiness and delay the subject of the sentence.

Powerful verbs create a word picture. They prompt a question in the mind of the reader. What story thought comes to mind when reading each of these sentences?

He came into the room.

He fell into the room.

He stumbled into the room.

He bounded into the room.

He raced into the room.

He strode into the room.

He sauntered into the room.

Sentences: It's All in the Details

There are various types of sentences and each conveys information to the reader in a different way. Varying the type of sentences in your manuscript will help the reader stay focused and add interest.

Here are four different types of sentences and their uses.

Controlling sentences: name and control the topic.

The prison was damp and cold. There was no concern for the inmates.

Clarifying sentences: help make the topic clearer.

Inmate comfort was not a top priority with the warden. It was no secret that his annual bonus was, in part, based on reduction in the cost of running the facility. Discussion of the utility bills took up a major portion of his weekly staff meetings.

Completing sentences: add specific details.

There was no air conditioning at the Cadejama Prison in Death Valley. The cells had no windows to open in the spring to dry the humidity, nor in the summer to relieve the oppressive heat. In winter, the indoor temperature never exceeded 40 degrees. The only attempt at climate control for the inmates came in December, with the issue of one thin, well-used blanket.

<u>Period Sentence:</u>   delays the most important thought and deliberately withholds it from the reader to create a special climax.

Subjected to marginal living conditions and confined in her cell day after day, she began to go mad.

      The first three sentence types are cumulative. They begin with the main clause and continue with details. The period sentence is more powerful because it offers known information at the start of the sentence, and saves the unknown detail for the end.

      Think of a sentence as shooting a gun. The bullet travels through the air, but where it stops is most important. Words travel through the sentence, but our interest is what they reveal at the end of the thought.

      The way we arrange words in a sentence brings our story to life, adds interest, and makes a significant impression on the reader. Sentence structure can make a good story great.

Word Wise

     Misused words not only distract the reader from the story flow, they detract from your intended meaning.
Here are some of the most commonly misused words and their meanings:
Accept: to receive
Except: a special situation, an exception
Affect: a verb, to influence
Effect: the result, the impact
Allowed: permitted
Aloud: an adverb, to be clearly heard
Ant: an insect
Aunt: a close female relative
Anxious: fearful, stressful
Eager: excitement, anticipation
Bare: unclothed
Bear: an animal
Board: a piece of wood
Bored: disinterested
Brake: part of a vehicle; to slow down
Break: something broken
Bring: to move toward another
Take: to carry away
Loose: (loos) free or untied
Lose: (looz) misplace; fail to win
Passed: move beyond an object or place
Past: previous to present time
Peace: absence of war
Piece: smaller part of a whole

Sit: be seated
Set: to place something
Sore: painful
Soar: accelerate
Stationery: a piece of paper
Stationary: stay in one place; unmovable
Than: used in a comparison
Then: sequence of time
Waist: body part
Waste: a useless item
Who's: contraction for who is
Whose: shows ownership

Writing Style: Syntactical Arrangement

Syntax – the study of the structure of grammatical sentences in a language.

Arrange – to place in proper, desired, or convenient order.

Words are the basic tools of the writer. They are the building blocks of sentences. Meaning is conveyed to the reader by the words chosen, the sentence length, and the placement of words within the sentence.

The order of words in a sentence does four basic things:

1) Conveys information

2) Makes a point of emphasis

3) Provides ease of expression

4) Creates a pattern for the flow of words

Read these examples to see and feel how the same information provides a different experience for the reader.

The girl ran quickly home.

Here the emphasis is on the speed of the girl's run home.

Quickly, the girl ran home.

This sentence conveys a sense of urgency about the girl's sudden decision to run home.

The girl quickly ran home.

This sentences emphasizes the girls need to get home as fast as possible.

Using the same words and sentence length, the meaning has been shifted by the use of syntactical arrangement—the order in which the words were placed within the sentence.

Improve your writing by arranging and rearranging the words in your sentences to convey your exact meaning to the reader.

About the Author

Valerie Allen is a psychologist, author, and speaker. She is in private practice and makes presentations for educators, mental health professionals, and writers. She is a member of the National League of American Pen Women and the Space Coast Writers' Guild. She is one of the founders of Authors for Authors.

She writes fiction, nonfiction, and children's literature. Her articles have been published in newspapers, online, literary publications, parenting, educational and mental health magazines. See *ValerieAllenWriter.com*

She has also published two novels, *Suffer the Little Children* and *Sins of the Father*. Her next novel, *Amazing Grace*, is forthcoming. A portion of the proceeds from the sale of these books is donated to domestic shelters. Her children's chapter books, *Summer School for Smarties* and *Bad Hair, Good Hat, New Friends* are for children in grades two to five. Her self-help book, *Beyond the Inkblots: Confusion to Harmony* is used by mental health professionals and those seeking support to decrease anxiety and discover how to take charge and move their life in a positive direction.

ORDER FORM

Write, Publish, Sell!
Quick, Easy, Inexpensive ideas for the
Marketing Challenged

ISBN 978 1480043855   *Cost $ 12.95*

Can be ordered from:
- *Online booksellers*
- *As an E Book*
- *Local bookstores*
- *The author: VAllenBooks@cs.com*

For an autographed copy with free shipping/postage, you may order directly from the author: Valerie Allen, P. O. Box 120053, West Melbourne, FL 32912-0053

Name: _____

Phone: _____

Address: _____

City: _____ *ST.* _____ *ZIP:* _____

Email: _____

Please send your comments to: *VAllenBooks@cs.com*
www.ValerieAllenWriter.com

Other books by Valerie Allen

Beyond the Inkblots: Confusion to Harmony

Suffer the Little Children

Sins of the Father

Summer School for Smarties

Bad Hair, Good Hat, New Friends

Made in the USA
Charleston, SC
29 October 2012